Queen Elizabeth II

Dorothy Turner

Illustrations by Richard Hook

Great Lives

William Shakespeare
Queen Elizabeth II
Anne Frank
Martin Luther King
Clive Sinclair
Helen Keller
Ferdinand Magellan
Mother Teresa
Louis Braille
John Lennon
John F. Kennedy

First published in 1985 by
Wayland (Publishers) Limited
49 Lansdowne Place, Hove
East Sussex BN3 1HF, England

© Copyright 1985 Wayland (Publishers) Ltd

ISBN 0 85078 494 8

Phototypeset by Kalligraphics Ltd, Redhill, Surrey
Printed in Italy by G. Canale & C.S.p.A., Turin
Bound in the U.K. by The Pitman Press, Bath

Contents

A baby Princess

On 21 April 1926, during the reign of King George V, a baby girl was born in an elegant mansion in Bruton Street, London. She was named Princess Elizabeth Alexandra Mary.

The baby's father was the Duke of York, the second son of King George V. Her mother was the Duchess of York. Both parents were delighted by the arrival of their daughter, who was their first child.

Soon the Princess's grandparents, King George and Queen Mary, drove to Bruton Street to see the new baby. They were greeted by cheering crowds. People were excited to learn of the birth of a royal baby, but no-one at the time knew that one day the Princess would become Queen. That seemed most unlikely to happen for Princess Elizabeth was only third in line to the throne.

First in line was the King's eldest son, the Prince of Wales. After him came the Princess's

The Duke and Duchess of York with their baby daughter

4

father, the Duke of York. And if the Duke and Duchess of York later had a son, he would take Elizabeth's place in the line of succession. She would move further and further away from the throne. But the unexpected did happen. Twenty-six years later, Princess Elizabeth Alexandra Mary became Queen Elizabeth II.

Little Princess Elizabeth with her mother

King George V and Queen Mary, the Princess' grandparents

Early days

For a short time the baby Princess Elizabeth continued to live in the house in Bruton Street where she was born. Years later, during the Second World War, the house was destroyed by German bombs. Now a bank has been built on the site, but a plaque on the wall indicates that it was the birthplace of the future Queen Elizabeth II.

Like all royal babies, the Princess was looked after by a nanny. It was the nanny's job to feed and dress the baby and take her out in her pram. Twice a day she would take the Princess to see her parents.

Comings and goings through the gates of Buckingham Palace in 1926

The Princess's family

Princess Elizabeth's father, then the Duke of York, later became King George VI. Her mother, the Duchess of York, is today known as the Queen Mother. When Princess Elizabeth was a baby, however, her parents did not know that they would one day bear the titles King and Queen.

When Princess Elizabeth was four years old, the Duchess of York had another baby – Princess Margaret Rose (now known more simply as Princess Margaret). Elizabeth decided to call her new

The Princesses out for a ride with their Nanny, Nurse Clara Knight

sister Bud. When asked why, she replied, 'Well, she's not a real Rose yet, is she? She's only a bud.'

Princess Elizabeth also had a nickname. In the family she was known as 'Lilibet', because that was the nearest she could get to pronouncing her own name when she was learning to talk.

Princess Elizabeth and her baby sister

7

Childhood

were spent at royal palaces such as Sandringham in Norfolk, or Windsor Castle, or Glamis, the Duchess's home in Scotland.

But privilege of this kind has disadvantages. Unlike most other children, the Princesses could not run out and play with friends when they wished. Wherever they went, crowds always collected. They had to be constantly protected from the 'outside world'.

Boisterous high spirits at a garden fete

The Princesses had a privileged childhood. So many people sent them presents that they had more toys than they could possibly play with. Elizabeth had her first riding lesson when she was only two-and-a-half. A year later she was given her own pony as a Christmas present.

Life was spent at various royal houses. The Duke and Duchess of York moved into a new house in London, in Piccadilly. Holidays

It was decided that Princess Elizabeth would not attend school. Instead, a governess was employed to teach her. The mornings were taken up with school lessons. The afternoons were free. Sometimes she had music and dancing lessons. At Windsor, at weekends, she could ride her pony. Evenings were often taken up with card games played with her parents. And, if it was difficult to have many friends, there were always pets. At one time Princess Elizabeth had ponies, corgis and fifteen budgerigars to look after.

The Princesses outside the play house given to them by the people of Wales

Occasionally Princess Elizabeth would go shopping with her sister and mother in London's big stores. Once a year she would be taken to the pantomime. Their governess once took the two Princesses on a London underground tube train – a strange and thrilling event for the little girls. But even this was not a real view of the 'outside world', for crowds and photographers soon gathered around them.

WAYNE SCHOOL

9

Three Kings

Early in 1936, when Elizabeth was nine, her grandfather – King George V – died. He had been popular and his death caused much sadness. His body was taken to the Houses of Parliament to lie in state. Princess Elizabeth, dressed all in black, was taken to see the coffin.

The new King was George V's eldest son, the Prince of Wales. Princess Elizabeth knew him as Uncle David, but he took the name Edward VIII when he succeeded to the title of King.

Many people were unhappy at the prospect of having Edward VIII as King. He did not seem the

King George V

King Edward VIII

dedicated sort of person that people had come to expect in their monarch and they thought he was unsuitable for the difficult and demanding job. When he fell in love with a divorced American lady called Mrs Simpson, and insisted on marrying her despite great opposition, he was strongly criticized by many people.

As a result, Edward VIII abdicated (gave up the throne) after only a few months. The crown passed to his brother, the Duke of York.

George VI leaving 10 Downing Street after a meeting with his Prime Minister

King George VI

Princess Elizabeth's father was a shy and gentle man who did not enjoy being in the limelight. However, he had a strong sense of duty. So he accepted the role of King and took the title King George VI. Within one year, England had three kings.

This meant great changes in Princess Elizabeth's life. When she saw a letter addressed to 'Her Majesty the Queen', she said, 'That's Mummy now, isn't it?' It was; and Elizabeth herself was now heir (the next in line) to the throne.

11

Growing up

Princess Elizabeth and Princess Margaret Rose in their robes at the time of their parents' coronation

The family moved to Buckingham Palace. The Princess's parents had wanted her to be brought up as much like other children as possible. Now, however, this was even more difficult to achieve.

A Brownie pack and Guide company were formed at Buckingham Palace, especially for the Princesses to join. They all met in a summerhouse in the palace gardens. These girls, together with royal cousins, formed the small circle of Elizabeth's friends.

As a young child, Princess Elizabeth had a rather solemn attitude to life. Now she was to be prepared for the difficult job of Queen, and she took her responsibilities very seriously. On 12 May 1937, her father was crowned King. Elizabeth and Margaret wore long robes and gold coronets. Elizabeth behaved with great dignity – and she made sure her sister did too. As Princess Elizabeth reported after the ceremony, 'I only had to nudge her once or twice when she played with the prayer books too loudly.'

It is said that if Elizabeth felt unwell she would try not to show it, saying that she 'must not take the easy way out'. Such courage and determination have stood her in good stead in later years.

But the future Queen Elizabeth had a good sense of fun, too. She especially enjoyed family games and entertainments. Each Christmas at Windsor, she appeared with her sister and their friends in pantomimes – Aladdin, Cinderella, The Sleeping Beauty – and she thoroughly enjoyed performing in these.

At times it must have been overwhelming to know that one day she would have to take on the heavy responsibility of being

Starring in the pantomime Aladdin, at Windsor Castle

The gardens of Buckingham Palace

Queen of Great Britain, Northern Ireland and the Commonwealth. No wonder Princess Elizabeth sometimes hoped that a brother would be born to take her place.

In the summer of 1939, when Princess Elizabeth was thirteen, she met Prince Philip of Greece. Philip was then eighteen and a cadet at naval college. Elizabeth and Philip were third cousins, both having Queen Victoria as a great-great-grandmother. It has been claimed that the Princess fell in love with Philip at their very first meeting.

13

War with Germany

But terrible events were about to shake the world. Two months after Princess Elizabeth and Prince Philip first met, Hitler's armies invaded Poland and the Second World War broke out. Britain was at war and was to remain so for the next six years.

The King decided that the Princesses should stay at Windsor Castle, although their whereabouts were kept secret from the public. Anti-aircraft guns and air raid shelters were installed.

In 1940, German bombs fell on Buckingham Palace while the King and Queen were in residence. Many areas of London were destroyed and the King and Queen toured the bombed streets, comforting the people.

Prince Philip was serving on a battleship in the Mediterranean. Already there were rumours of a possible romance between the Prince and the heir to the throne. Princess Elizabeth, too, wanted to play some part in the war. So, when she was eighteen, her father agreed to her joining the ATS

Learning to change a wheel in the ATS, during the war

(Auxiliary Territorial Service). There she learned how to repair cars and lorries. For a short time she became 'No. 230873 Second Subaltern Elizabeth Alexandra Mary Windsor'.

Peace

Many people in Europe had suffered terribly during the war years. Finally, on 8 May 1945, the war ended with Germany's surrender. On that evening the Royal Family appeared time and again on the balcony of Buckingham Palace. Crowds cheered and cheered with delight. Later that night, Princess Elizabeth and Princess Margaret slipped out to mingle, unnoticed, with the dancing crowds. It was a rare moment of freedom.

The Royal Family and Prime Minister Winston Churchill wave to the delighted crowds

Engagement and marriage

Princess Elizabeth and Prince Philip became engaged in the summer of 1946, while on holiday at Balmoral, but a public announcement of their engagement was not made until the following year.

In the meantime, King George VI, the Queen and the two Princesses visited South Africa. While they were there, Princess Elizabeth celebrated her twenty-first birthday. In a radio broadcast she dedicated herself to her future subjects, saying:

'I declare before you all that my whole life, whether it be long or short, shall be devoted to your service . . .'

Two months after her return from South Africa, the public were told of the engagement. The wedding would take place later in the year and soon presents were pouring in from all over the world. Prince Philip was given the title of Duke of Edinburgh and, in November 1947, he and Elizabeth were married. Once again crowds cheered in the streets as they celebrated. The ceremony and splendour of the royal wedding took many people's minds off the poverty and grimness of post-war Britain.

In November the following year Prince Charles, their first child, was born. Then, in August 1950, he was joined by a sister – Princess Anne.

The engagement of Princess Elizabeth to Prince Philip

Elizabeth becomes Queen

Princess Elizabeth's father, King George VI, had been in poor health for some time, although he was only fifty-six years old. When he suddenly died on 6 February 1952, Princess Elizabeth and her husband were in Africa.

Treetops, in Kenya, where the Princess became Queen

Queen Elizabeth II is greeted by senior members of her government, as she arrives back in Britain

The Princess, who had spent the night watching wild elephants and rhino at the Treetops Hotel in Kenya, was told of his death. It was a sad and solemn moment. Straight away she prepared to fly back to London. Princess Elizabeth was now Queen.

The Coronation

After mourning for the dead King, preparations began for the Coronation of Elizabeth II.

For a while the whole country seemed to be gripped by 'coronation fever'. When the great day arrived, 2 June 1953, the pavements of London were packed with people camping out, waiting for a glimpse of the Queen and the Coronation procession as it made its way from Buckingham Palace to Westminster Abbey. It rained all night, and most of

In the Golden Coach

Coronation Day itself, but nobody in the huge crowd seemed to mind, for the British people were out to enjoy themselves.

The ancient crowning ceremony in Westminster Abbey was solemn and moving. Seated on a throne, the Queen was presented with the symbols of majesty – the orb, sceptre, rod and royal ring. Then the Archbishop of Canterbury raised the heavy Saint Edward's Crown into the air and slowly lowered it on to the Queen's head. Shouts of 'God Save the Queen' swept through the Abbey. Trumpets sounded, the Abbey bells rang and throughout London guns were fired in salute.

For the first time, these events were watched by a huge television audience. T.V. was only just beginning to be part of people's lives. Few had sets, but all over the country groups shared a place together in front of the small, black and white (and often fuzzy) screens. For many, it was the first time they had watched T.V. and it made their day even more exciting and memorable.

The Queen's work

Since that day in 1953, the Queen has worked continually and tirelessly for her country. Her strong sense of duty to her many subjects throughout the United Kingdom and the Commonwealth has never faltered. But what *is* the job of a king or queen in our modern world?

Long ago, their job was to rule the country, to defend it against enemies, and to make the laws. But modern British monarchs do not have this power. The Queen does not govern the country – Parliament does that – but without her approval no new law can be made. No-one can become

Trooping the Colour

prime minister until the Queen has invited them to form a new government. A new session of Parliament cannot begin until the Queen has officially opened the Parliament in an elaborate ceremony.

Every day government papers and reports appear on the Queen's desk, carried in special boxes. It is her job to read them all. It is said that she spends about two hours of *every* day reading them through.

Each Tuesday evening the Prime Minister goes to visit the Queen to discuss the latest political situation. Prime ministers have often remarked on how well-informed the Queen is, and several times they have been caught out when the Queen has known more about a particular topic than they have!

Arriving for an official visit to Saudi Arabia

In addition to these duties, the Queen makes constant public appearances – in factories, schools, hospitals – and has won the hearts of many of her subjects by going on informal 'walk-abouts' among her people. Once a year she takes the salute at the Trooping the Colour ceremony in London.

Just as important are her visits abroad. There she represents the whole British nation and plays a part in Britain's friendships with other countries.

Shortly after the Coronation, the Queen and Prince Philip went on the longest royal tour ever made. For almost six months they travelled, by boat and plane, right round the world, visiting Commonwealth countries. Since then the Queen and her family have made many journeys abroad.

Reading documents is a daily task

21

Private life

A family group

In February 1960 the Queen had another son, Prince Andrew. Four years later she had a fourth child, Prince Edward. In the midst of all the official duties, family life has always been very important to her. And there *are* breaks in the official duties. She takes six weeks off at Christmas, four weeks at Easter and ten in the summer. These breaks give the Queen some much-valued time with her family.

In 1969, the Queen agreed to a film being made about her family. It was called simply *Royal Family*, and it was shown on television. Millions of viewers were given glimpses of the Queen, her husband and children, at work and doing ordinary things, such as picnicking on holiday at Balmoral. The film was a huge success.

The Queen's love of horses and dogs is well known. It is said that she is at her happiest relaxing with her family, in the countryside, with dogs at her heels and a stout pair of wellington boots to protect her feet. She is also a very good horsewoman and likes to keep fit by riding. She has her own racing stable and one of her greatest pleasures is to watch racing, especially when one of her own horses is taking part.

Once, when she was a young princess, Elizabeth was asked what she would like to be when she was grown up. She replied 'a lady living in the country with lots of horses and dogs'. When her other duties allow, that is just what the Queen still likes to be.

Enjoying a ride on her horse 'Agreement'

WAYNE SCHOOL

The Silver Jubilee

The Queen walks through the City of London with the Lord Mayor, after celebrating her Silver Jubilee at St Paul's Cathedral

In June 1977, Queen Elizabeth II had reigned for twenty-five years. June 2 was her Silver Jubilee. A thanksgiving ceremony was held at St Paul's Cathedral and celebrations were held throughout the country. People held parties in the streets and lit bonfires and fireworks. It seemed clear that the British people liked having a monarch, and they particularly approved of the way Elizabeth II was carrying out her work as Queen.

A modern monarchy

In the 1960s, however, the Royal Family had been criticized for being 'stuffy' and out of date. That can hardly be said to be true today, for the Queen has ensured that the monarchy has changed with the times.

The Queen and Prince Philip made sure that their children attended schools, and so were not sheltered from the world as the Queen herself had been in her youth. Both Prince Charles and Prince Andrew have served in the armed forces – Prince Andrew was a helicopter pilot in the Navy

A scene from the film Royal Family

during the Falklands War. Princess Anne has won international awards for her horse-riding. Prince Edward has taught at a school in New Zealand.

The Queen has also helped to soften some of the more fixed ideas of the past. She has been prepared to show the world some of the details of her private life (as in the *Royal Family* film) and has met many of her subjects on 'walkabout' – often at risk to her own safety.

In carrying out her duty to her people, the Queen frequently has to put her own feelings to one side. Her task is a difficult one, often made more difficult by prying newspapermen.

On a 'walkabout' in South-East London

25

Heir to the throne

Prince Charles in special robes for his introduction into the House of Lords

Prince Charles is the Queen's eldest son and therefore heir to the throne. As Prince of Wales, he represents the Queen on many occasions, all over the world. He controls extensive farmlands in the Duchy of Cornwall, in the south-west of England. Prince Charles has served in the Royal Navy, commanding a minesweeper. He is an enthusiastic diver and has himself helped to recover treasures from the sunken Tudor warship *Mary Rose*.

For a long time people had wondered whom Prince Charles would marry. The Queen, and the British people, were delighted when he married Lady Diana Spencer (now the Princess of Wales) in 1981. When their first child, Prince William, was born in the following year, the new baby ensured that the royal line would be continued.

It has been suggested that the Queen might one day step down from the throne to allow the Prince of Wales to take over as King. This would make sense,

above: *The newly-weds leave St Paul's Cathedral*

right: *The Prince and Princess of Wales with their eldest child, Prince William*

say, if she were very old or ill. But it would be a break with tradition, and the Queen does not think of her work as being 'just like any other job', with a retirement age.

If all goes according to plan, Prince Charles (and then his son Prince William) should be crowned kings in succession to Queen Elizabeth. But will the British system of monarchy survive that long?

The future

The Queen talks to a group of Guides and Brownies in Scotland

In the past two hundred years, many foreign monarchs have had to give up their thrones. Their people have decided instead, to choose their ruler. Many leaders, such as prime ministers and presidents, are voted into office for a limited number of years only. Kings and queens, of course, inherit their titles for life and cannot be voted 'in' or 'out'.

Queen Elizabeth II is one of the richest people in the world. Even so, having a monarchy costs money. Critics of the Royal Family say that we should not spend so many millions of pounds of taxpayers' money (over £15 million a year) on the Queen and her large number of relatives.

Supporters of the monarchy, however, point out that having a king or queen has helped maintain safe and steady government in the United Kingdom. They also argue that the Queen and other members of the Royal Family do invaluable work for the country. They help to promote good relations with the Commonwealth and many other countries, and this, in turn, boosts Britain's trade.

And, in any case, most of the British people *like* having a Royal Family. King Farouk, ex-King of Egypt (one of the countries that overthrew its monarchy) once said he thought that by the end of the twentieth century there would be only five royal houses left: those of Clubs, Diamonds, Hearts, Spades and Windsor – Queen Elizabeth's family! But the Queen has made it clear that if the people of the United Kingdom wanted to end the system of monarchy, she would consider it her duty to step down. At the moment this seems a very remote possibility indeed.

Four generations of the royal family attend Christmas service at St George's Chapel, Windsor

Family tree

Queen Victoria = Prince Albert

King Edward VII = Queen Alexandra

King George V = Queen Mary

King Edward VIII   King George VI = Queen Elizabeth

Queen Elizabeth II = Prince Philip   Princess Margaret

Prince Charles =   Princess Anne   Prince Andrew   Prince Edward
Princess Diana

Prince William   Prince Henry (Harry)

New words

Abdicate   To resign; especially to give up the throne of a country.

ATS   The Auxiliary Territorial Service – now the Women's Royal Army Corps.

Commonwealth   The British Commonwealth of Nations: a group of separate countries united by close ties to Britain. Many member states were once British colonies.

Coronet   A small crown.

Heir to the throne   The next in line to the throne. The person to whom the throne, property (or a title) passes when the previous holder dies. Prince Charles is heir to the throne of the United Kingdom.

Jubilee   A joyful celebration; a Silver Jubilee celebrates 25 years of a reign; a Golden Jubilee celebrates 50 years.

Lie in state   When the body of a monarch or other important person is displayed so that mourners can pay their last respects.

Monarch   A king or queen.

Monarchy   A nation governed by a king or queen; a system of government that has a king or queen at the head.

Orb   The golden globe, studded with jewels, used in the Coronation ceremony.

Sceptre   The golden staff carried by a king or queen as a sign of authority.

Books to read

All about the Royal Family by Phoebe Hitchens (Macmillan, 1983)
Her Majesty the Queen by Ian A. Morrison (Ladybird Books, 1983)
Queen Elizabeth II by Alan Hamilton (Hamish Hamilton, 1982)

Index